BOOK MARKETING 101

AN INTRODUCTION TO THE WORLD OF BOOK MARKETING

Heather Hart

Body and Soul Publishing

Colorado Springs, CO

Shelley Hitz
P.O. Box 6542
Colorado Springs, CO 80934
www.trainingauthors.com

Earnings Disclaimer: There is no promise or representation that you will make a certain amount of sales, or any sales, as a result of using the techniques that are outlined within this book. Any earnings, revenue, or results using these marketing strategies are strictly estimates and there is no guarantee that you will have the same results. You accept the risk that the earnings and income statements differ by individual. The use of our in-formation, products and services should be based on your own due diligence and you agree that we are not liable for your success or failure.

Full Disclosure: Some of the links in this book may be affiliate links (excluding any and all links to Amazon) and we may earn a small commission when you make a purchase through them. By law (FTC), we must disclose this. However, we want to ensure you that we only endorse products and services we believe in and would or do use ourselves.

Book Layout ©2013 Book Design Templates
www.trainingauthors.com/booktemplates

Ordering Information:
Quantity sales. Special discounts are available on quantity purchases by corporations, associations, and others. For details, contact the "Special Sales Department" at the ad-dress above.

Book Marketing 101 / Heather Hart. – 1st ed.

Printed In The United States of America

ISBN- 13: 987-0615649368
ISBN- 10: 061564936X

TABLE OF CONTENTS

FOREWORD

When I first started publishing books in 2008, I did so to help teen girls struggling with body image and self-esteem. I had no idea that several years later I would be earning a full-time income publishing print books, eBooks, and audiobooks. However, I have learned a lot along the way—unfortunately, most of it the hard way.

I launched my first website for authors in 2010 to help authors get self-published and market their books with success. I wanted to share what I had learned (and continue to learn) about self-publishing and book marketing.

Along the way there have been many people that have helped me. However, the one person that has helped me the most, and that I often think of as my right hand woman, is Heather Hart. She has co-authored several books with me. She has also edited and formatted many of my books. I was so impressed with her work that I asked her partner with me in the work I do to help authors at TrainingAuthors.com.

And so I introduce you to Heather Hart. Much of what we have learned along the way, we have learned together. I think you will learn a lot from Heather as she shares with you valuable book marketing tips in this book....tips I wish I would have known when I first started self-publishing books.

We are cheering you on!
Shelley Hitz,
Best-selling author and owner of TrainingAuthors.com

A Gift for You!

Before you dig in to the information in this book, we want to give you our training, "Building a Book Marketing Plan," a $27 value, free of charge.

Why?

Simply because we enjoy helping authors succeed.

In this training, you will download our master book marketing plan template with a PDF training report.

Claim your free copy at the link below:
www.trainingauthors.com/freegift

<u>Book Marketing:</u>
The art of promoting one's book to gain exposure
and increase sales.

Alternate definition:
A term that makes authors squirm

About Book Marketing

Most authors are writers by nature; however what to do with the book once it is written does not come quite as naturally. When we find out the only way to sell the book we have written is to market it, it can be tempting to run for the hills. Even if we are up for the challenge, many of us don't have a clue what we are actually supposed to do. So we do what we know—scream out to the world about our book with the hope that someone is actually listening. We tell our friends and our family, we post about it 1,000 times a day to our Facebook and Twitter accounts, but we still don't see the results that we long for. Well, I am here to tell you that there is a better way—and you don't have to run away screaming.

Book marketing should be a planned process, an art if you will. It takes patience and the perusal of goals. Only if you keep at it will you truly be successful. I once heard of it compared to childbirth: the writing process is like pregnancy, the publishing, birth, and the book marketing would be the child rearing—and I believe that there is truth to that. When we are writing our books, we are nurturing them so that they can grow strong and develop into the books we know are inside of us. But even during that writing stage, we should be preparing for their arrival as well. Letting people know that they are coming, and preparing a place for them in our lives—marketing starts even before our books are published. Just like expecting parents prepare for their baby, most experts say that you should start marketing your book 6-9 months before it is released. Don't panic if you don't have that long, it is just something helpful to know for next time. Essentially, it is *never* too early to start marketing your book.

However, the majority of our marketing efforts will occur after the process of writing our books is completed. Publishing is tedious labor, but even once it is completed, our work has only just started. Once our book is published, or born if you will, we have the privilege of announcing it to the world. We get to help it spread its metaphorical wings and fly.

Before You Start

Now, before you get too excited about seeing your book fly up the best-seller ladder you need to remember that while marketing your book is the act of letting potential readers know of its existence and convincing them to read it, it starts long before most authors realize it. Part of marketing your book is selecting a catchy title, eye-grabbing cover, competitive price, and adding an interesting blurb on the back cover which all work together to draw the reader in. You can tell readers about your book until you are blue in the face, but without the above things, they aren't very likely to take the bait.

It is also important to your book marketing efforts to make sure that you can get your book registered with major distributors. Some publishing companies will do this for you, but others will require you to do it yourself. This is something that you will want to consider before you even publish your book.

For instance, if one of your major goals is to see your book on the shelves at Barnes and Noble, you will want to make sure that your publisher is not an imprint of Amazon. So if you are going with CreateSpace, you will need to purchase your own ISBN so that you can be listed as the publisher.

Shall We Begin?

My hope is that you find this book helpful in your book rearing journey, but just as with parenting, I can only give you tips for the trail, what you actually end up doing us ultimately up to you.

CHAPTER ONE

Building Your Brand

According to Wikipedia.com, a brand is a "name, term, design, symbol, or any other feature that identifies one seller's goods or services as distinct from those of other sellers." If we want people to recognize our work, we have to have a brand—however, there is no set requirement for building your brand. When building your brand, you could use a special font or color pallet, create a logo, trademark, or slogan, or any number of different tactics—it really is up to you, but building a brand is important. Even something as simple as your author photo can become part of your brand. For authors, our writing style, or voice, will also contribute to the way that we are identified by our readers.

The most important thing to remember is that *your brand needs to be about you*. Don't go for what you think your readers want to see, or what is trending when you are setting it up, keep it about you. Some of the best author branding that I have seen has somehow invoked the author's character. Maybe it was that the author was laughing in their author photo or the vibrant colors of their website, it was just totally them, and it stuck.

The more of you that you put into building your brand, the more of an impact it will have.

With a good brand, you will no longer be just another author on the block—you will be a real person with real style. That is what you are going for. You want your brand to be memorable, and to be _you_.

The Different Aspects of Branding

While your brand is not made up of just one thing, it is important to pay close attention to each aspect of your brand. It is something that will be used to identify you, so you want to make sure it is sending the right message. Here is a list of some of the things that you will want to consider when building your brand:

Tagline

What is your purpose? Or what passion do you want to be best known for? Is your writing driven by your principles, beliefs, or enthusiasm? Who are you trying to reach? These are all questions that you should consider when creating your tagline. You need to decide what your main focus will be when promoting your book and then word it in one or two sentences that you can share easily—something that you can incorporate into your "about the author" sections as well as short bios to accompany articles or profiles on various web pages. This will become your tagline—or mission statement if you will—the more focused it is, the better of an idea you will have of how to successfully fulfill (or live up to) it when marketing your book.

You also want your tagline to be distinct and unique. When people see your brand, this is the message that you want to run through their mind. And vice versa—if they hear the message, you want your name to pop into their heads. This should be the impression that you want people to have about you and your work all summed up into a short, yet powerful, blurb.

When creating a tagline, you might want to do some keyword research to make it as powerful as possible. Using keywords and phrases can ensure that you rank higher in search engines. You can do keyword research on Google and even sign up for Google alerts to see when your tagline or keywords are showing up on the internet.

Screen Name

Will you use a pen-name, your real name, the name of your book, blog or series, or something else entirely to identify yourself? Each site that you sign up for will ask for a display name. Try to choose a name that will be available on multiple sites as your screen name and avoid using something that is popular and less likely to be available. Another factor is its length—is it so long (or so short) that sites won't accept it? Think long term and try to foresee any issues that you might run across.

Your screen name will be a big part of your brand. You will want it to be something fairly consistent that people will be able to find when searching through different sites, and something that they can associate with you. You might want to think twice about using your high school nickname if it is not something that portraits you as a professional, or does not aid in the message that you are trying to establish about yourself.

This should also be the domain name that you have for your website, or related to it. If people type in YourScreenName.com you want to make sure that they find you, not a realty company or rival author.

Depending on your budget, I recommend purchasing your domain as early as possible; you might also consider purchasing the .net and .org versions as well as any common misspellings to make sure that your brand is protected.

I also recommend registering it in some of the popular free sites as well such as Blogger, WordPress, and blog.com. Protecting your brand is huge, and with all of the book mimicking going on today, you want to make sure that people who are looking for your book find you, and not someone who is mimicking your work.

Author Photo

Don't just slap a photo of yourself on your profile(s)—it's best to make sure that your author photo is a picture that you want people to relate to you. Pay close attention to the background, what you are wearing, what you are doing... Do you want just a mug shot, or do you want a picture of you reading a book, writing, or enjoying a different hobby?

Size is also an issue; you will want something that looks good both really small, but also in larger sizes. Pay attention to the pixels as well as whether or not the photo will be able to be cropped if needed.

The Look

You need to add some personality to the look of your brand. Whether you are coming up with a logo or just a design scheme, this is something that you will want to touch all aspects of your personality. What is your favorite font? Your favorite color(s)? Your favorite thing to do or your favorite place to be? This should be something that you can apply to your blog, website, business cards, etc.—make it something that you can adapt to fit other places when the need for design arises.

Your author photo should mesh well with this look (or vice versa), so you might want to consider that when picking it out.

Your Voice

As an author, your writing voice will play a huge part in your brand. While it won't be as immediate as the rest of your brand, it will have an impact. I remember reading a book a few years back and I kept checking to see who the author was because it sounded just like a much more popular one that I was very familiar with. Kudos to the much more familiar author because I recognized his voice... even when someone else was using it. You don't want to be the author on the other end of that though. I still don't remember who it was—I just know it wasn't who it sounded like.

Your voice will also be the determining factor for some readers. There are several authors that I won't read because I don't like their writing style. They write fabulous books, some of which are on the best-seller lists, so obviously there are people who do like their voices, I'm just not one of them. Likewise, there are authors who I love that others don't care for. Find your voice, and stick with it. Switching voices won't gain you more readers, it will just push away the ones who thought they liked you.

One Last Branding Tip

The most important thing to remember is that your brand should be about you. Don't research what's trending, this is something that you want to reflect yourself as an author. It should be something that is timeless and can stick with you for your entire writing career, however there is no law saying that you can't change it if it's not working for you. Just remember that the more you change it, the less it will be known.

CHAPTER TWO

Creating a Presence

Once you've got your brand, it is time to start making your presence known. You want people to know who you are and what you do—*and* you want them to come to like and trust you. That sounds obvious, but I can't stress enough that you shouldn't shout out your existence from every platform that you find. Creating a presence is about networking and relationship building.

Relationships will be one of the biggest book marketing tools that you have. The bigger and better your presence, the more people you will potentially reach. But remember—bigger isn't always better. Don't shout just to be heard, people don't want another crazy author spamming their inboxes, blog feeds, etc. Your goal is to build connections. Trust me, you don't want to be the one that shows up at the party and takes over by telling everyone how great they think they are—because while you are busy singing your own praises, everyone else will be busy tuning you out. Instead, be social and get to know others. Use whatever platforms you can to connect with likeminded people and build relationships.

There are lots of different platforms through which you can build your presence. So many in fact, that you could probably spend the rest of your life trying to take part in them all—I don't recommend doing that. The best idea is to build your presence slowly, adding more platforms as you master current ones and have the time. After all, the last thing you want to do is to spend all of your time networking, and not have any time to write.

7 Types of Platforms

<u>Social Networks</u>

Pretty much anyone and everyone these days is involved in some sort of social media, and it seems like more social sites are being created every day. Popular social networking sites include Facebook, Twitter, Google+, and Pinterest. However, once again, I don't think that I could ever mention them all.

Social networking is a great way to build your online presence. If you really want to connect with others, this is a great way to do it. And again, I recommend starting with one or two, and adding more as you are confidently established in those.

If you are new to the world of social media, you can find some great tips and tutorials on my website at:
http://trainingauthors.com/bookmarketing/#socialmedia

<u>Forums</u>

Forums are another great way to build your presence. If you are ever looking to connect with like-minded people, forums are the place to do it. You can join forums about writing, or forums that are related to your specific niche. Some of the more popular forums for writers are LinkedIn, Kindle Boards, and the Absolute Write Water Cooler. You can build your presence by asking thought provoking questions, or giving insightful answers to other people's questions.

Forums are both give and take, the general rule of thumb is that you should never take more than you give.

Blog/Website

Creating a blog is a fabulous way to give others the opportunity to keep up with you. It takes relationships a bit deeper than social networking by allowing followers deeper into your thought processes. You can blog about the writing life, your books, character profiles, short stories, or anything else that your little heart desires.

Websites and blogs are also great places for others to fall in love with your writing. If you can keep them hooked on weekly (or multi-weekly) posts, they will be more likely to put out the money to purchase your work. Blogs also help you stay disciplined as a writer by providing self-imposed deadlines—posting regularly will make your blog more valuable to the readers, so if you vow to post every Monday, you will have accountability to your readers to stick to it.

Blogging also builds your presence in a way that nothing else can. If you pay attention to SEO (Search Engine Optimization) and do a little keyword research, your blog/website will give you a higher probability of showing up in search engines—which means that more people will be driven to your site to see what you have to offer.

The best part? You can blog for free! Most people recommend purchasing your own domain, but while beneficial, it's not required.

There are also a few sites out there that let you create a website for free—although any free domain name will not look as professional as a .com, .net, or .org. so I recommend at the very least paying for the domain name. You can find my blog post about building your own WordPress website from scratch at:

http://www.trainingauthors.com/building-an-author-website/

That being said, I cannot stress enough that building your presence through your blog or website should not be one sided. The goal is not just to be seen, but to build relationships. Let people comment on your posts—and then respond to them. Share your e-mail address on your website or include a form that people can use to contact you—I personally used EmailMeForm.com's free contact form on my first blog. It was on Blogger, but now I have switched to WordPress I use a free plugin instead.

Virtual Book Shelves

These are becoming more and more popular among readers. With Goodreads leading the way, Shelfari and others are coming up fast. They provide readers a place to connect with one another, and with their favorite authors. Becoming well known in these online hangouts is an idea worth having.

Virtual bookshelves provide a place for readers to discuss their favorite books and connect with other readers that read the same things they do. If you write fantasy books, you might join some virtual book clubs and connect with fantasy readers. Once you have built relationships with some of the members there, you can let them know that you are working on a book of your own that they might enjoy reading.

Author Hangouts

If the readers are hanging out at Goodreads and Shelfari, the authors should have hangouts too, right?

Absolutely! There are tons of online communities for authors such as the Author's Den; a quick Google search will turn up several so I recommend adding your niche. For instance, if you are self-published you might want to check out IndieAuthors.com, but no matter which hangout you join, they are all great places to meet other authors.

The other thing about author hangouts is that they provide a place where you can get questions answered about writing in your niche. You can bounce ideas off of other authors and sometimes even get feedback on your work. The other important thing to note is that most authors are also readers, so if you can get them excited about your book, there's a good chance that they will want a copy when it comes out – especially if they put effort into helping you.

Your Own E-mail List

While you are working on building your presence, take notes—start building an e-mail list. Whether you send out monthly newsletters to let your following know about your publishing progress, blog posts, etc. or use it to share your writing is totally up to you, but building an e-mail list is not a platform that you can afford to skip out on.

When building your e-mail list you can offer a free gift for signing up (which is one of the most popular ways) and/or you can describe the benefits that people who subscribe will receive to encourage people to join. It is a good idea to place a sign up form (or links to it) on multiple pages of your website so that it is easy for people to find, as well as to ask whatever following you have to let their friends know about it.

Just remember that people's inboxes are full already, so only send out messages when you have something important to say, and if you are sending out weekly or monthly e-mails (which can be a good idea) make sure that the content is actually beneficial to keep your followers engaged. If all I get from someone is sales pitches, I won't be signed up to their list for long, but if you are providing content that I find helpful, yours will be one of the few that I actually read each month.

There are multiple e-mail service providers. I've used several in the past, but you can find out what I'm currently recommending at: http://www.trainingauthors.com/recommendedemail

Join Organizations

Search out organizations (both on and off-line) in your niche that you might be able to become a part of. Volunteer your time to help them with a project or become a member of their group. This will help you build relationships that have a solid foundation. Imagine their delight when they find out that you have written a book! You won't even have to make a pitch if you have done a good job working with them.

The Bottom Line...

The bottom line in any of the above platforms that you can use to build your presence, is that no one likes a one sided relationship—it's got to be both give and take. If you are writing a blog, let people comment—encourage people to comment. If you are sending out e-mails, make sure that you respond to any responses that you get in return.

Once you have built your presence, you can't forget about it. Maintaining it is a must, otherwise it was all for not. There are some great free tools out there that can help with this—my personal favorite being Hootsuite which allows me to schedule tweets and Facebook posts to go live at a later time or date. This way even when I'm not online, I'm still present. It also helps me to space out my posts so that I can share multiple posts without cluttering my follower's feeds.

The other tool that I would recommend is Klout. Klout is a great way to learn how to optimize your presence. It gives you a score that updates daily. If you want to test out different ways to spread your influence, it will help you to see if those ways are working.

Ready? Go, build your presence, maintain it, and optimize it—Be social!

CHAPTER THREE

Internet Marketing

This is where all of that networking pays off. Each and every online connection can be converted into a book marketing tool. So all of the time you spent creating your presence really makes a difference here. It is practically impossible to successfully market your book online if you aren't present online. It is also hard to create that presence when you are more concerned with sales than with relationships. That's why it is important that you build your presence *before* you begin marketing.

Online Marketing Platforms

Most of these will probably look familiar to you, but each one is best utilized in its own way. Just like when you were creating your presence, you don't want to attack them all at once, but ease in gently gaining a firm grasp on each one before moving to the next. It's better to do one thing well, then ten things poorly.

Blog/Website

Your blog or website should be the hub of your internet marketing efforts. Virtually every other platform that you use online, should link back to this. Thus, it must be used to promote your book. There are several different ways you can market your book from your blog or website, the most obvious way would be to include information about your book on the sidebar, landing page, and/or a static page. You can also write blogs about your book from time to time, or add updates to your website about your publishing success. You might include a sales page right on your blog, or an affiliate link to your book on Amazon (if you aren't signed up as an Amazon affiliate, I recommend doing so now provided you don't live in an area that is excluded from their program).

You may also want to consider adding a media room to your website that contains press releases, previous appearances you have had in the media, sample interview questions, book synopsis, graphics people can use when promoting your book, and anything else you want to provide others access to—make it easy for them to share about you!

Social Media

This is the number one way that authors market their books online, and I cannot stress enough that you should not spam your audience with messages saying "buy my book!"—that is a sure fire way to lose ground. Instead, use social media to engage your readers and share updates about your publishing processes or new book reviews. You can share quotes from your book or ideas for a new one. Be creative.

We already talked about building your presence in social media, but each social media site has its own book marketing perks.

Twitter allows you to host Twitter parties to create buzz about your new book, or use hashtags to reach other twitter users that are not in your direct following.

Facebook has author pages and even allows you to set up your own book store right there on your page.

There are entire books out there that have been written solely about the use of social media in marketing your book. Why? Because it has amazing potential, and you can use it to share almost all of your other book marketing endeavors. You can tweet about a press release that you just posted, or invite your Facebook friends to a book signing that you are having next week. Simply letting your following know what you are up to is a powerful way to expand your book marketing efforts.

Forums

Many forums allow you to add a signature to your post. You can use this to mention your book or even link to it or your website when allowed. Bare minimum you should add information about your book to your forum profiles. Make sure that you are providing helpful answers to people and not just spamming boards with information about your book—never answer a forum question by saying you answered their question in your book. You can give a short answer and say that you went into more detail in your book, but don't just pitch your book and run, be helpful.

Press Releases

There are a growing number of places online where you can submit a press release about your book for free and there are also a number of places where you can spend hundreds of dollars to promote a press release online. Make sure you know which one you are doing before you sign up.

You can write a press release whenever you do something new. You can announce that you are expecting to release a new book in x number of months, that you just released a book, that you are having a book launch, that your book sales reached an all-time high, and so on and so forth.

While press release sites monitor releases to make sure that they are newsworthy, there are still several different newsworthy reasons to write a press release, and even the free press releases will show up in Google searches and gain you more exposure.

Blogs that are Not Your Own

You don't have to have a blog to write one. Guest blogging is a great way to reach more people. You can write guest posts when you see an opening, or plan a virtual book tour and schedule multiple posts in a row on several different blogs. Each blog that you have a post published on is like free publicity to their following. You can write a post related to your book or niche, or something entirely different and include your book information in your bio. Most blog posts stay up forever, so this is free lasting marketing.

The most important part though, is that if you tell someone that you will write a post for them, follow through and do good work. Don't leave them hanging and don't provide something that you didn't put your best into.

Video Sharing Sites

Have you thought about creating a book trailer? I made one using the free software that came on my computer with quotes from the book and royalty free images and music. It was simple and free.

You can also record yourself reading part of the book or talking about what inspired the book, basically anything you can write about you can make a video about, and in each video description you can put a link to your book or website.

Podcasting

Similar to video sharing, podcasts are a way to use audio to promote your book. With sites like Speaker.com, you can simply record a message that you want to share with your readers/ potential readers, and then provide them with a link to it. Or you could record a sound bit with the free Audacity software on your computer and embed it on your website.

Once again, you can record yourself reading a segment of your book, or talking about something related—it is totally up to you and the options are endless.

Virtual Bookshelves

Many authors use virtual bookshelves to host question and answer sessions or to form book clubs for their books, but you can also use these platforms for giveaways or writing blog posts.

Remember, this is where readers hang out—your potential buyers—the more exposure you can gain here, the more sales potential you will have.

Author Hangouts

Many author hangouts have places where you can list the books that you have written. You can also add your books to your profile, and let the authors that you have gotten acquainted with know that your book is finally out. It is however important not to spam the community, or break any of the rules. Always check the community rules before posting about your book.

I actually find the best use of author hangouts is for networking with other authors, and sharing about each other's books. So that is something else you might consider.

Book Previews

There are several sites out there like 1ChapterFree.com where you can upload one chapter of your book for people to read. This is a great way to hook your audience and let them know whether or not they will be interested in your book—BookBuzzr.com provides a widget that allows readers to go through part of your book, turning the pages as if it were real—it's pretty cool, and you can add it right to your website!

You can also share portions of your book using Google Docs, 4Shared, writing a Facebook note, in a blog post, or including a sample page on your website. All of these have the same marketing function: to convince readers that your book is worth buying by giving them a taste of it.

Your Own E-mail List

Remember that e-mail list that you started building? It's now an amazing marketing tool! You can e-mail your list to let readers know about book promotions, when you release a new book, a special that you are having, or just to let them know about a positive review.

Personally, I have seen some amazing results from my e-mail list. By sending out an e-mail to let them know about a giveaway that had ended resulted in skyrocketing sales for the month. All I did was add a link in the e-mail to let those who didn't win know where they could purchase a copy.

E-mail lists work!

Don't forget to add your book information to your e-mail signature or link to your website where they can find information about it.

Other Online Marketing Strategies

Book Reviews

When you are spending money on something, do you want to know that the product is what it says it is? Of course you do. It doesn't matter if you're purchasing a new printer or spending money on a book. With the number of books out there to choose from, reviews can either make or break the sale. After all, wouldn't you rather buy a book that other people have read left feedback on then spending money on something that you have to take an unknown authors word on? Even a bad review is better than no reviews—though good reviews are your ultimate goal.

Tip: Smashwords.com allows you to create coupons that you can use to gift copies of your book to potential reviewers, or you can also send a free copy to some of the people on your mailing list in exchange for an honest review. When giving out free review copies, you might want to include a note asking your reviewers to disclose that they got a free copy of the book in exchange for an honest review to be in accordance with the Federal Trade Commission's 16 CFR, Part 255: "Guides Concerning the Use of Endorsements and Testimonials in Advertising."

You can learn more about getting reviews for your book "How to Get Honest Reviews"—a book I co-authored with Shelley Hitz. You can find that online at: http://www.trainingauthors.com/books/honest-reviews/

Article Submissions

Submitting articles is similar to guest blogging, only often times you can even get paid for it. You can write articles for websites, magazines, your local newspaper, or even for a newsletter. Again, make sure that you meet your deadlines and put your best foot forward.

When considering writing an article, you will want to research the market and find out what submission guidelines you must meet. Sometimes you have to submit your article idea for approval before they will even look at your actual work. It's important to know the guidelines before proceeding.

To find writing markets in your niche and their guidelines you can do a quick Google search or check with your favorite magazines or local newspaper. Worldwide Freelance has a list of writing markets that you might want to look into. You can't access their entire list without signing up, but even the ones that they share in their free newsletter or on their public site can give you some ideas.

Teleseminars and Online Conferences

Hosting teleseminars and online conferences using tools like Instant Teleseminar is a great way to gain exposure and promote your book. They allow you to get to know your audience in a whole new way while establishing yourself as an expert in their eyes all at the same time.

Even fiction authors can benefit from these by using them for question and answer segments or to tell the story behind the book. They can be used to real your readers in just as much as establishing yourself as a professional.

A great free tool that I use and recommend is Google Hangouts. They are awesome because the recording is automatically uploaded to your YouTube channel. You can learn more about them at: http://www.trainingauthors.com/how-to-host-a-live-webinar-for-free-using-google-hangouts/

Author Interviews

Similar to guest blogging, author interviews are a great way to market your book. You can do an interview about your publishing method, marketing success, your book, the list of possibilities could go on and on. Sometimes people will approach you to ask about interviewing you, but you can also seek out sites that do author interviews and inquire about being interviewed on their site.

Freebies

Free stuff is a great way to win your readers over. While there are tons of people out there who just collect free stuff because it's free, there are plenty of others out there who actually use it. You can use free reports or short stories as bonus gifts when people sign up for your e-mail list or when they purchase a copy of your book, or you can donate them to other people in your niche to giveaway for you— just be sure to include information about your book somewhere inside of them.

You can also host contests or sponsor giveaways. This method is a highly successful way of marketing books. It can be costly to give away print versions of your book, but you can give away a PDF via e-mail for free (minus the time), or even issue a Smashwords coupon to cover the cost. People tell their friends about free stuff, so if you can give something away for free that is valuable, you will in the end be gaining more exposure and receiving free marketing through all of the people who shared about it with their friends and following.

CHAPTER FOUR

Leaving a Paper Trail

While internet marketing has the potential to reach people far out of your physical realm, traditional marketing shouldn't be written off. Creating and leaving a paper trail can be a successful book marketing strategy. We see thousands of names and images on the internet each day, and while some of those sites are added to our favorites, they all stay on the computer and are forgotten when we are out actually living our lives, which is why paper trails can only add to your marketing efforts, going where the internet cannot.

Business Cards

Having a business card should be a must for every author. You can use these in different ways, but they are physical reminders that you are an author. They can contain information about your books, or even just web addresses to where they can learn more about who you are and what you write. The branding on your cards should match that of your website.

There are tons of ways to hand out business cards. We have all seen the restaurants that have the bowl for business cards on the front counter. They use these to know who is in their community, and we want them to know that we are here! You can include them in cards or letters to family and friends, or simply hand them to strangers on the street who inquire about what you do.

There are lots of places online where you can order business cards at a low cost. I highly recommend reading reviews and checking to make sure that you know what you are going to get. Most of these places also offer templates that you can update with your information if you cannot afford to get one professionally designed, or if you don't have the knowhow or connections to get a design done on your own.

Brochures/Handouts

Brochures and other handouts can come in many shapes and sizes. You can have a postcard, a tri-fold brochure, a flyer or a small booklet. The point of these is to take your prospective audience further than you can with a simple business card. You could include your author photo and short bio, book information, positive reviews, and links. You might even include an excerpt from your book.

Bookmarks

You wrote a book right? Why not make a bookmark to use in it? This will take a bit of designing skills, but you can probably find a template online. Include the name of your book and a link to your website, and then drop a handful off at your local library. You could spice it up with a quote from the book or a positive review, but even something simple will get the job done.

Posters

I love posters. With the growing number of public places that have community bulletin boards, these are a must. You should be able to create a simple poster on your own with just the information about your book and the cover image. Then add some tabs that they can tear off on the bottom, and voila! You have a great marketing tool that you can post at the library, coffee shop, or anywhere else that you see an open board. You can also print posters to see about hanging in windows of places that don't have boards.

I recently heard of an author that made a poster for a café that he visited weekly offering their customers a discount if they bought his book. "Written by one of our own" is what I believe it said.

Media Kits

While a lot of media contacting is done via the internet, it is always a good idea to be prepared. Having a physical packet to give out can give you a leg up over the competition. You can create media kits for radio stations, T.V. studios, or other organizations. A standard media kit might include a letter of introduction, your business card, a fact sheet, testimonials, bookmarks, about the author section, a method for them to respond to you (phone number, e-mail address, or self-addressed stamped envelope) and possibly a DVD with your book trailer, an author spotlight or an audio clip. You can also include a request form for them to place orders for additional media kits, books, bookmarks, etc.

While having a standard media kit prepared is amazingly helpful, you also want to be sure to do your research and tailor your kit to whomever you are sending it to. Perhaps if you are sending it to your favorite radio station you can include a Smashwords coupon so that each of the DJ's can download it for free. If you are sending it to a television station within your niche, you might want to include a DVD with a short clip about the book in case they decide to promote it. You will also want to include a personalized letter describing why you are sending them your media kit, how it will benefit them, and what all is included.

You can spend quite a bit of money to have a media kit professionally designed, or you can simply make one on your own and slip it into a folder. Just make sure that it looks professional and connects with your audience.

Direct Mail

If you have already created marketing material, why not mail it out? It will cost a little bit for postage, but you can mail your brochure, bookmark, and business card to organizations in your niche, or mail your media packet to a radio station.

Remember Aunt Emma? Why not send her a letter letting her know that you are a published author with some bookmarks so that she can brag to her friends?

Snail mail might not be popular anymore, but it still makes the person on the receiving end feel special. You might also want to check out SendOutCards.com as they will even send out the mail for you to make it simpler. You can't include your bookmarks that way, but you could include a message about your book.

Taking it Further

The best part about a paper trail is that it doesn't have to stop with you. You can e-mail your poster design to friends and family that live out of town to see if they will hang some up for you, or get them some bookmarks and/or brochures to pass out.

You can also use your paper trail to boost your internet marketing success with QR codes. You can get a free QR code at http://goqr.me/, and once you have it, you can have it printed on the back of your business cards and add it to your posters, brochures, bookmarks, etc.

CHAPTER FIVE

Adding a Personal Touch

Once you have got the following, the tools, and the experience marketing your masterpiece, it's time to add the personal touch. There are so many ways to do this! In fact, the sky is the limit when adding a personal touch to your work. It can be as simple as changing the voicemail message on your phone to include something about your book (e.g., "You have reached Sally Smith, author of 'Because You Called'…") or something much more in depth like setting up an event.

So, are you ready to get up and stretch your legs and start hearing the sound of your own voice? I hope so, because adding a personal touch to your marketing efforts can really be the icing on the cake.

Warning—it is important to note that coming out of your writing shell and embracing your audience can either make or break your career. You want to be professional, approachable, and likeable. You don't want to reach out and touch someone if you haven't showered for over a week. Remember to be polite, speak like an author, and be friendly—smile!

Phone Inquiries

It is amazing what a simple phone call can do. As long as your book is carried by a distributor like Ingram, then calling bookstores can go a long way. Simply pick up the phone and dial, when they answer let them know you are an author, ask them to check your ISBN to see if they carry it, then ask if they would place an order to carry some in stock. I have heard of authors having great success with that method.

Another thing that phone calls can accomplish is setting up a time to meet with the person in charge of choosing which books to stock, learning about consignment options, or even simply finding out about events hosted by the book store that you might be able to become a part of—some of these things can be accomplished via e-mail, but putting a voice behind your inquiry makes things a bit more personal.

Door-to-Door Marketing

After placing some phone calls or doing some internet research, why not set aside some time to visit bookstores in your area? After all, if a phone call is more personal than an e-mail, how much more personal is a face to face meeting? You can also use this opportunity to drop off some bookmarks for them to hand out to their customers or see if they have a community board where you can pin up a poster about your book.

You might need to check prior to going to a store to see if they discourage unsolicited sales calls, if it's stated on their website that any unannounced visits are prohibited, it can actually do more harm than good. If they do prohibit you from speaking face to face with them about your book, it might still be a good idea to go in and check out the store to see if it would be a good fit for your book. Your e-mails or phone calls will make more of an impact if you can let them know that you have actually been to the store and can make them more personalized to the store instead of sounding like a general mass e-mail inquiry.

Book Clubs

Are you part of a book club? If so, why not ask if they can read your book next? If not, you can still seek out some book clubs and ask them if they would consider using your book. You might offer them a discount for ordering their books through you, or a question and answer segment with you after they have read the book.

Organize Events

A great way to promote your work is by getting to know others in your niche, and one of the best ways to do that is through local events. You might consider organizing a meet and greet for local authors, or a fundraiser to support a local charity.

You can also look into setting up book signings at a local book store, or a book reading at your local library. I highly recommend that no matter what kind of an event you are setting up that you bring a treat to share. A bowl of chocolate kisses (or carrot sticks) will lure people your way and give them sweet memories of their time with you.

Consider Public Speaking Engagements

Shelley Hitz wrote her first book so that she would have something to leave behind after speaking engagements, but it can go the other way too. If you want to promote your book, you might consider setting up a speaking engagement or ten. These should be related to your books niche, but you can speak in schools, churches, libraries, or other organizations. Do you write children's books or books on parenting? Check out the local MOPS group. If you write about fishing, check with the local fisherman's association. While you're inquiring about speaking engagements, don't forget to leave a paper trail!

Pay it Forward

I cannot tell you how many books I have sold without even trying by just offering to help another author or by volunteering my time to help out a ministry or organization. Once the person/group finds out I'm an author, they want to know more and ask me about it—I don't even have to make a pitch!

The bottom line is that when you help others, they want to help you too. If your book doesn't apply to them, they might purchase it for a friend or at the very least pass on your information.

CHAPTER SIX

At a Higher Cost

While the number of free and low cost options for marketing your book on a shoestring budget are numerous, a book about book marketing wouldn't be complete without mentioning some higher cost options that are available. If you have the money and want to reach more people, you might consider one or more of the following options...

Purchasing Ads or Sponsorships

The obvious first step to a high dollar marketing campaign would be purchasing ads or sponsorships. Depending on where you want to place your ad, will determine just how expensive this will be. You can purchase ads on websites, in newspapers and magazines, or even on signs if you feel the need.

While the definition of advertising and sponsorships overlap to a certain degree, there is a difference. Generally a sponsorship is more personal than an advertisement. Advertisements are usually just a money exchange, while sponsorships go a bit deeper. The difference is best scene in little league baseball. You can purchase an ad to be placed on the score board, or you can sponsor the team and have your name printed on the back of each of the player's jerseys. In one, you simply have an ad that can be scene, while in the other you have a personal representation of your company. I don't know of any authors who have advertised with little league, but hey, if that's your niche it could happen. If baseball isn't your niche, there's still hope. You can sponsor all kinds of events—both on and off-line, as well as teams, radio shows, T.V. programs, or anything else that offers the option.

The most common type of advertising purchased by authors, is online marketing. Sites like Ereader News Today, BookBub, and Kindle Daily Nation.

Putting Together Promotional Packages

If you want to have a book launch or a special promotion, you might consider putting together prize packs to promote the event. Sometimes you can get others to support your event and provide prizes free of charge (or in exchange for a copy of your book or a service that you provide), but other times you have to front the cost yourself.

You can also be on the other side of that, and donate a copy of your book to someone else's prize pack to gain exposure.

Creating an Affiliate or Reward Program

This is probably one of the most overlooked marketing strategies that is out there, but with good reason. Programs that offer rewards or incentives are either extremely beneficial or extremely costly. There is rarely a middle ground.

While there are several different types of Affiliate programs, the most popular work on a commission basis. For each sale that an affiliate refers they earn part of the money from that sale. Lots of major companies like Wal-Mart and Amazon use affiliate programs.

Rewards programs on the other hand, work on a point system. Customers can earn points by purchasing products, referring new customers, or even by helping you publicize an event or promotion. They can then use those points for a discount off of their next purchase or for free prizes that you offer.

Both are great ways to get others to help you market your book; however they each come at a price.

Create Your Own Gear

There are several print on demand companies that allow you to design your own gear. This can be virtually free if you just post a link to it on your website and allow fans to order their own, or you can use it for promotion and it might get a bit more costly.

If you are going to a speaking engagement or setting up a booth at a fair, you might consider having buttons made to take with you that say "I love books by 'your name'" or something along those lines. Or if you are putting together a promotional package, you might want to include a t-shirt or a mug with your tagline, logo, a quote from your book, or something else on it that would double as marketing for you, and then maybe you could package it all nicely in a personalized book bag? Perhaps for Christmas you can make a shirt for your mom that says "My Child is an Author—Read his/her Books" with a QR code or link to your website or book title.

Those are just a few of the many ideas that are possible when you create your own gear. Plus, once you come up with a design that you like, you can have it printed on multiple mediums.

Hire a Professional

Outsourcing can be extremely expensive, but it doesn't always have to be. You can sometimes get people to volunteer to help you or exchange services to get something done.

You can hire someone to market your book for you, or just to help you with part of your marketing plan. For instance you might hire a designer to help you design your business cards or website, or a book marketing specialist to manage your campaign. If you can't stand the thought of social media, you might want to look into hiring someone to do that for you so that you don't miss out on that part of your online presence. Or if you like social media, but have no clue how to manage a website, you could hire that part out. How much or how little of your marketing you want to pay someone else to do is totally up to you, but with the growing number of book marketing specialists and firms online today, the option is definitely there if you're interested.

Attend a Writing Conference

Writing conferences are a great way to make connections and learn more about writing, publishing and marketing. Many of them also offer the opportunity to sell your books while you are there.

Generally, writer's conferences are not cheap, however if money is an issue, you might check to see if they have scholarships available or even start a crowdfunding campaign. While you are there meeting new people and selling your books, you can also checkout any workshops that they have on book marketing or writing in your niche.

CHAPTER SEVEN

Making a Plan

N ow that you know many of the different options available for marketing your book, it's time to make a plan. I'm sure that you have all heard the saying, "If you fail to plan, you plan to fail." Well, that is extremely true when it comes to marketing your book. Without a plan, you will never know if you hit your goals or even if you are moving in the right direction.

When making your book marketing plan, there are a few different things that you will want to look at. Each book should have its own plan, and be tailored to the author's goals for that particular book. Here's a list of some of the things to consider when making your plan:

What is the Goal?

Before you can even start planning, you have to know what your goal is. For some authors, their sole goal is to see their book on the shelves at Barnes and Noble, other authors want to make a living off of their books and could care less where they are sold, still other authors just want people to read their books and location and income are not factors. You have to know what your goal is before you can figure out how to achieve it.

When deciding on your goal, you will want to make sure that it is specific, measurable, attainable, realistic, and timely—or S.M.A.R.T. If your goal isn't specific enough, it will be harder to know if you are actually moving in the right direction. For instance, 'to sell books' isn't really specific, and while you can measure whether or not you're selling books, how will you know when you have attained your goal? You could revamp that goal to 'selling 100 paperback copies of your book within 3 months'. That would help you to direct your marketing efforts into promoting the paperback version vs. the eBook (provided you have both). Likewise, if this is your first book it's probably not realistic to make your goal to be on the N.Y. Bestsellers list within 6 months. Perhaps a better idea would be to start small and work up, you could start by going for number one in your category on Amazon.com, and work up from there.

The last thing you need to know about setting a goal is that it doesn't have to be set in stone. While it's crucial to have a goal, it's totally okay to change your goal if needed. Let's say you hit number one in your Amazon category within a week, you can up your goal, or if you see that your original goal isn't really what you wanted or isn't reachable, you can decide to shift your focus to a new goal.

Define Your Target Audience:

You might already know the answer to this, but who do you want to buy your book? This will be the people that you want to concentrate your marketing efforts on. Does it make more sense marketing a cookbook to college boys or to middle aged women? Sure there are

BOOK MARKETING 101 | 51

tons of college guys that like to cook, but you will probably get more sales from the women. Note that even if you are concentrating your marketing efforts on moms with young children, you are not limited to that audience alone. If you have a college in the area you can absolutely check with the faculty about marketing your book there, it just probably shouldn't be the main focus of your marketing efforts. Alternatively, if you have written a book about surviving your freshman year of college, the college might be exactly where you want to focus your marketing efforts and resources.

Determining your target audience will help you get the most return out of your marketing efforts, but once again, if you see that your book is being bought primarily outside of your target audience, you can change it if you need to.

What is Your Budget and Timetable?

If you are working on a shoestring budget—purchasing an ad in Writer's Digest is probably out of the question.

Are you already working on your next book? You probably don't want to spend all of your time marketing, and have no time left for writing.

Before you can create your plan, you have to know how much time and money you have to work with. Book marketing has the ability to eat up both if you're not careful, so writing down exactly what you have to work with will prevent you from ending up exhausted and broke.

And while book marketing is a never ending process for the author, you will want to set a specific book marketing timetable. I recommend a six month book marketing plan as you should be able to plan in advance how much time and money to put into your marketing for six month increments, but you can do shorter or longer plans if you so desire—you are the one doing the work after all!

Create Your Action Plan:

Once you have determined your goal, target audience, budget and timeline, you are ready to make a plan! The first thing you will want to do is to break your goal up into smaller goals. If your goal is to sell 100 books in three months, you might have a one month goal of selling 50 books and then 25 books each month after that. If your goal was to be on the Amazon best seller list, your smaller goals might lead up to putting together and executing a successful book launch.

Once you have your smaller goals defined, you can work on deciding which marketing tactics you will use to let your target audience know about your book so that you can achieve those goals.

You can get my book marketing plan template free at: http://www.trainingauthors.com/freegift

One More Thing:

You might have noticed the above theme—flexibility! Having a plan is key to your marketing success, but it should not be set in stone. Planning gives you direction and ensures that you stay on course, but if your destination changes or a roadblock is thrown into your path, don't stop—alter your course and continue on!

CONCLUSION

I want to close this book by encouraging you to think outside of the marketing box and come up with new ways that you can expand your book marketing efforts. For example you might connect with other authors to promote each other's work (with mentions in books, reviews, or website link exchanges) or even to donate your book for a giveaway, to be part of a prize package, or to a library or doctor's office. The sky is the limit and as long as you want to market your book, there will always be new possibilities. Keep at it and your work will pay off. Remember, start small, create a plan, follow through, and branch out whenever *you* are ready.

You might have noticed that I mentioned numerous tools and resources in this book, but TrainingAuthors.com has even more tools and resources available that will benefit authors who are marketing their book(s). You can find our list of tools we use and resources we recommend at: http://www.trainingauthors.com/resources/

The one thing that I haven't mentioned yet is the importance of tracking your book marketing success. You need to make sure that your work is yielding the return that you hoped for. If you purchased an ad and didn't see any increase in sales, you know that you probably don't want to do that again. If people are subscribing to your e-mail list just long enough to download whatever you're offering for free, you might want to evaluate the content that you are sending out, and so on and so forth. Tracking your success will help your book marketing efforts to be even more successful.

And the best book marketing tip that I could give you is *simply publishing more books*. Publishing more books gives your already satisfied customers another option—most people would rather buy from an author that they already know and trust then someone new. Plus, you can also mention your first book in your second book, and your first and second books in your third book, etc., or when marketing additional books you can include that you are also the author of such and such.

The process of book marketing is a cycle. It will never be completed unless you are ready to stop selling books. You start with a vision, make a plan, execute that plan, evaluate your success and then improve your plan to come up with a new vision and make a new plan to execute, evaluate and improve. You can constantly add or subtract different marketing efforts with the goal of coming up with what works best for you.

I hope that you have found this book helpful in your book marketing endeavors, and I wish you success on your marketing journey.

~ Heather

A Year of Book Marketing

MARKETING YOUR BOOK ONE DAY AT A TIME

by Heather Hart

SUCCESSFUL MARKETING

Once you have a foundation for your marketing, it's important to use that foundation as a springboard to successful marketing—taking it from ordinary to extraordinary. To truly market your book successfully, you not only need to know what you are doing, you also need to have the tools to get you there and an action plan to keep you where you want to be. One of my favorite quotes is:

"If you fail to plan, you plan to fail."

I believe that if we really want to be successful at something, we have to have a plan. It isn't always the amount of time it takes that makes something great, it's simply a matter of maximizing the time we have. And let's face it, in today's world time is one of the things that we all lack the most!

Helpful Tools

Before we get too far, you need to know about some really cool tools that will help you successfully market your book. There are hundreds if not thousands of free and paid tools available online today, but there are 3 that I couldn't market my book without – well, not successfully anyway.

<u>Hootsuite</u> – Hootsuite allows me to schedule posts on both Twitter and Facebook in advance. I can set them for a specific day and time, and then work on something else. This is helpful because I can post about an upcoming sale I'm having, or even schedule some generic promo posts, so I'm not trying to do everything every day. I generally spend an hour on Wednesdays scheduling posts for the coming week. I still log into Twitter and Facebook, but if I get really busy, I know that I'm still being represented there.

<u>Gremln</u> – Similar to Hootsuite, Gremln lets me schedule posts in advance – but the cool feature about Gremln is that they let you schedule your posts to repeat. So if you've got some generic marketing posts, you could have them automatically be sent out every 15 days or on the first Wednesday of every month – maybe even once a year. This is a huge time saver for me. I find Hootsuite's interface a bit easier to read, but you could get by with just Gremln as it does pretty much everything Hootsuite does.

<u>Bit.ly</u> – Bit.ly is awesome for shortening links. If you want to link to a blog post with a super long URL, or you want people to be able to remember your link easily, bit.ly can help you with that. For instance, bit.ly/21Devos is the link to one of my devotional books on Amazon. I've committed that to memory and I don't have to pull up the URL if I need to give it to someone. bit.ly/BookMarketing101 is the affiliate link to one of my marketing books. That's much easier than http://www.amazon.com/gp/prod-uct/061564936X/ref=as_li_ss_tl?ie=UTF8&camp=1789&crea-tive=390957&creativeASIN=061564936X&linkCode...etc. etc., don't 'cha think.

Weekly Marketing Habits:

The following is a list of things that I recommend getting in the habit of doing to market your book daily. Forming good habits – even small ones – can really make marketing easier for you in the long run. We touched on doing a few things routinely in the last chapter; this is what my routine marketing looks like – feel free to alter it to best fit your needs:

<u>Monday:</u> Brainstorming/Developing – Think of a new marketing activity (or work on one you haven't finished yet) such as creating a YouTube video, setting up a blog tour, build traffic for your website, host a contest, giveaway, or blog party (the possibilities are endless!) that you can focus on during the week and do some of the ground work.

<u>Tuesday:</u> Networking – Visit and/or join forums for authors or readers that are related to your niche. Finding one or two active forums that you enjoy, can be a great way to build a name for yourself and even pick up new readers – just make sure you read the forum rules before you start promoting your book. You can also use this time to read blogs by other people in your niche or writing blogs. Make sure to leave comments wherever you go so you work on building your online presence and actually form connections.

<u>Wednesday:</u> Social Media – Setting aside one day to schedule posts for times when you won't be online during the next week can save you a ton of time and help you to get more exposure. Writing tweets for past blog posts, book reviews, or promotional posts about your book to keep on hand and schedule throughout the week, month, or year, is a great way to stay on top of your marketing.

<u>Thursday:</u> Networking – Networking is important, so I highly encourage you to visit the forums/blogs twice every week.

<u>Friday:</u> Blogging – If you have a blog, spend time updating it at least once a week. If you don't have a blog, you can use this day to write articles or posts that others can publish or post on their blogs for you.

<u>Weekend:</u> If you want to market your book 365 days a year, then you'll need to work the weekends too (unless you have deemed scheduled posts or advertisements to qualify as marketing activities for the weekends). I generally set aside the weekend for research and writing time. This is when I write articles, guest posts, and current WIP (works in progress), as well as perform any market research that I need to do.

No matter what your marketing habits look like, it's really important to have them. Sitting down at a certain time every day and spending 30 minutes or so on marketing, is probably the best habit you could ever form as an author.

Planning

Besides the base habits and routines, it's important to plan out your marketing campaigns and activities. I keep a calendar with a record of blogs that I'm supposed to be hosted on, blog tours, sales, etc. so that I don't have a week when I'm totally frantic trying to do 3,000 marketing things. While if you're doing a book launch scheduling several things at once can be a good thing, normally you'll want to space your marketing campaigns out so you're not drowning. Instead of marketing your book with 5 campaigns in February, you can plan a few of those for March, or you might notice that you don't have anything scheduled for April and decide to push one back until then.

Another important aspect of planning your marketing in advance is that that you won't be rushed trying to throw together a blog tour in under a week. Planning one for 3 months down the road will help you deliver higher quality work and maintain your sanity.

Don't forget to plan for the future by saving a record of all your marketing e-mails, blog posts, press releases, and other material. If you go on a marketing campaign, the next one will be easier if you can rework material, or at least have a reference for what you did that did or didn't work. It's also helpful for sales that you might repeat year after year. Did you send your following an e-mail suggesting that they give your book as a Christmas gift? Save it so you can edit it and send it out again next year – cutting your work time in half for that promotion.

The goal presented in "A Year of Book Marketing" is to master marketing through persistence. Find out more about this book at: http://www.trainingauthors.com/books/a-year-of-book-marketing/

ADDITIONAL RESOURCES

Book Marketing Survival Guide Tool Kit

Access our database of templates, trainings and more with our Survival Guide Tool Kit. Find out more here:

www.trainingauthors.com/toolkit

Our Books for Authors

We have an entire library of books for authors, including books on publishing and marketing. Check out the entire list here:

www.trainingauthors.com/books

Recommended Outsourcers for Authors

If you need help with the technical side of publishing and marketing your books, consider outsourcing to one of our recommended providers here:

www.trainingauthors.com/recommended-outsourcers-for-authors

Tools and Resources We Use and Recommend

Check out the tools we use and recommend for writing, publishing and marketing here:

www.trainingauthors.com/resources

THE BOOK MARKETING SURVIVAL GUIDE SERIES

Are you fighting to survive the journey of marketing your book?

If so, we invite you to gear up with the Book Marketing Survival Guide Series.

Ranging in topics from how to run a book launch, to networking, to offline marketing, this series has something for every author—no matter what stage of the book marketing journey you are in. Each survival guide has a matching toolkit available where authors can access templates, checklists, video tutorials and more on the topic covered in the book.

Find out more at:

www.trainingauthors.com/books/#SurvivalGuides

ABOUT THE AUTHOR

Heather Hart is a book marketing expert, internationally best-selling author, and is the manager of multiple websites. With the heart of an author, Heather enjoys working from home where she spends her days typing away at her computer, brainstorming new marketing ideas, and encouraging those around her.

Her desire is to help others successfully publish and market their books while continuing to author, contribute to, and market multiple book marketing and faith-based books herself – and have fun doing it.

Heather works with Shelley Hitz at TrainingAuthos.com to help authors succeed. They have been working together since 2009 and have been referred to as the "writer's dynamic duo". One of the ways they help authors is by sharing their about their own experiences in the book industry.

Access Shelley and Heather's FREE Author Training at:
www.TrainingAuthors.com/Newsletter

See a Complete List of Their Books for Authors at:
www.TrainingAuthors.com/Books

Connect with Shelley and Heather Online at:
www.facebook.com/trainingauthors
www.twitter.com/trainingauthors
www.youtube.com/trainingauthors